Spotter's Guide to

# BIRDS
of North America

Dr Philip Burton

Special Consultant
Dr Kenneth Cooper
Assistant Professor, Division of Natural Sciences,
City University of New York

Illustrated by
Trevor Boyer and Tim Hayward

With additional illustrations by
Andy Martin

# Contents

Edited by Karen Goaman, Alice Geffen and Sue Jacquemier

**Library of Congress Cataloguing in Publication Data**
Burton, Philip John Kennedy.
  Spotter's guide to birds of North America.

  Includes index.
  1. Birds – North America – identification.
I. Title.
QL 681.H64 598. 2′ 97 79-730
ISBN 0-8317-0875-1
ISBN 0-7460 11.45 8.

Printed in Great Britain.

Possum Grape
13.95  4/03

# How to use this book

This book will help you to identify some of the birds you will see in North America (both in the USA and in Canada). Take it with you when you go looking for birds. The pictures show the birds standing, perching, flying or swimming, depending on how the bird is most often seen.

The male of each kind of bird is always shown. In many cases where the female is very different from the male, the female will be shown too. ♂ means male and ♀ means female. If a bird's plumage (feathers) changes from season to season, both kinds of plumage are shown.

The description next to each bird tells you where to look for it and also gives its approximate average size in inches. The measurements given for most birds are taken from the tip of the beak to the tip of the tail (see diagram). Very long-legged birds such as herons and egrets are measured by their

height from head to foot when standing. Birds on the same page are not always drawn to scale.

On the next page you will find a picture showing the different parts of a bird. There is also a list of special words and their meanings on page 63.

Each time you see a bird, check it off in the small circle next to the picture.

---

## Where the birds are found

You can find out the areas of North America in which each bird may be found by looking at the letters at the end of each description; they stand for the following areas:

**B** = **Both** Eastern and Western regions
**E** = **Eastern** region
**W** = **Western** region
**N** = **North**
**S** = **South**
**NW** = **North-West**
**NE** = **North-East**
**SW** = **South-West**

Often more than one of these letters will be used: e.g. **B(N)** means

that the bird is seen in both Eastern and Western regions, but mostly to the North of those regions; and **E(&SW)** means that the bird is seen in the East and also in the South-West.

Look at the map on page 57 to see how these areas are defined.

## Scorecards

There are two scorecards at the end of the book, one for the Eastern and one for the Western region. You will find a score for each bird you see in either region. You can add up your scores whenever you like, either after a day out spotting birds, or at the end of a vacation, for example.

## Where to look for birds

You can start birdwatching in your own backyard or from a window in your home. Try putting out food and water to attract the birds (see pages 52-5 for information and suggestions). When you get to know the birds near your home, you may want to look for different birds. You can look in a nearby park. Ponds, rivers, beaches, fields and woods are all good spots for birdwatching. Even old gravel pits, garbage dumps and swamps attract birds. The best time to go is early in the morning; early evening is also good. If you take a vacation you will be able to visit new places (different habitats) and see new species of birds. When you know the names of some birds you may want to know more about them. There is a list of books to read and clubs to join on page 56.

## Binoculars

You do not necessarily need binoculars to watch birds, but as you become more experienced you may want to buy some. Look for a light-weight pair. You should try several types. The best sizes are 7 x 35 or 8 x 40.

## Notebook

It is a good idea to keep a notebook. In it you can record the birds you see. Describe (or draw) new birds. This will help you to identify them later.

## Parts of a bird's body

These words will help you when you are reading the descriptions in this and other books about birds.

Crown

Forehead

Chin

Throat

Shoulder

Breast

Side

Belly

Tail feathers

Back

Rump

Wing bar

Secondary feathers

Primary feathers

Flank

**Yellow-rumped Warbler**

4

# Loon, Grebe, Pelican, Gannet

### Common Loon ▶
Breeds by inland waters of Canada and Alaska; winters on all coasts of North America. Flies with neck sloping down. Listen for eerie, laughing call. 32". B.

Summer

Winter

**Seldom flies**

**Floats high in water**

### ◀ Pied-billed Grebe
Found on shallow inland waters. Dives frequently. When alarmed, sinks slowly instead of diving. 13". B.

### Brown Pelican ▶
Seen on coastal waters, mainly in the south. Flocks fly in lines. Dives from flight for fish. Young are pale brown all over. 50". SE & W.

**Neck is white in winter**

**Has powerful flight with frequent short glides**

**Often glides on long, narrow wings**

### ◀ Gannet
Eastern bird seen on rocky offshore islands. Fishes by plunging into sea from up to 50' high. Young are dark gray with white spots. 37". E.

# Cormorant, Swan, Egrets

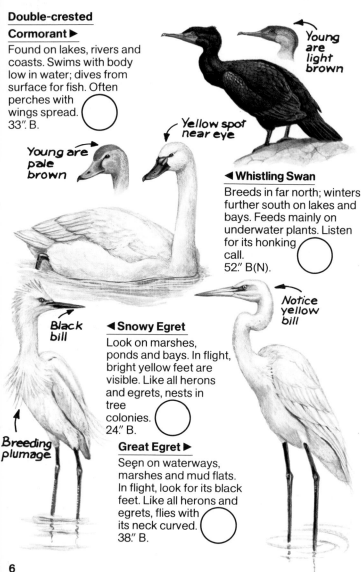

### Double-crested
### Cormorant ▶
Found on lakes, rivers and coasts. Swims with body low in water; dives from surface for fish. Often perches with wings spread. 33". B.

Young are light brown

Yellow spot near eye

Young are pale brown

### ◀ Whistling Swan
Breeds in far north; winters further south on lakes and bays. Feeds mainly on underwater plants. Listen for its honking call. 52". B(N).

Black bill

### ◀ Snowy Egret
Look on marshes, ponds and bays. In flight, bright yellow feet are visible. Like all herons and egrets, nests in tree colonies. 24". B.

Breeding plumage

Notice yellow bill

### Great Egret ▶
Seen on waterways, marshes and mud flats. In flight, look for its black feet. Like all herons and egrets, flies with its neck curved. 38". B.

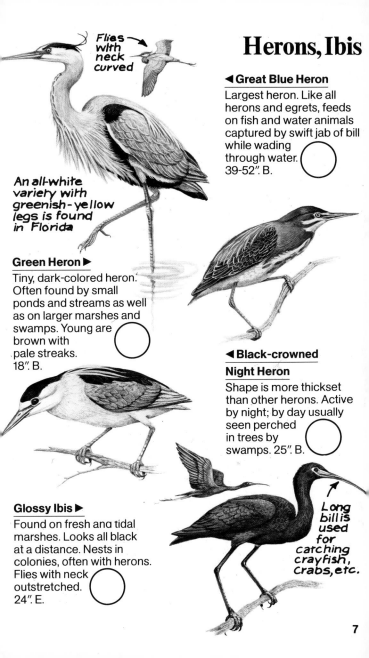

Flies with neck curved

An all-white variety with greenish-yellow legs is found in Florida

# Herons, Ibis

## ◄ Great Blue Heron

Largest heron. Like all herons and egrets, feeds on fish and water animals captured by swift jab of bill while wading through water. 39-52″. B.

## Green Heron ►

Tiny, dark-colored heron. Often found by small ponds and streams as well as on larger marshes and swamps. Young are brown with pale streaks. 18″. B.

## ◄ Black-crowned
## Night Heron

Shape is more thickset than other herons. Active by night; by day usually seen perched in trees by swamps. 25″. B.

## Glossy Ibis ►

Found on fresh and tidal marshes. Looks all black at a distance. Nests in colonies, often with herons. Flies with neck outstretched. 24″. E.

Long bill is used for catching crayfish, crabs, etc.

# Geese

Brant

### Canada Goose ▶
Several races, varying in size; some have darker bodies than others. Loud, honking call. Flocks fly in V-formation. Feeds in fields near water. 22-45″. B.

### Brant ▶
Feeds on the shore in bays and estuaries. Flocks fly in wavering lines. 17″. E.

Canada Goose

### ◀ White-fronted Goose
Habits similar to Canada Goose, but nests only in the far north. Has a high pitched, "yodelling" call. 28″. B(W).

White belly

*Orange legs*

Blue Goose

Snow Goose

### Snow Goose ▶
Breeds in Arctic; winters mainly on coastal bays and salt marshes. High pitched, barking call.

### Blue Goose ▶
A darker bodied variety, seen mainly in the west and on Gulf coast; both forms may be seen together in mixed flocks. 26″. B.

*Black wing-tips show in flight*

Mallard   Black Duck   Pintail   American Wigeon

# Ducks

Speculum

♀

♂

## Mallard ▶

This and the next six ducks are called dabbling ducks; they feed from the water surface or by "up-ending," but do not dive. Speculum is blue. 23". B.

♀

♂

## ◀ Black Duck

Like Mallard in habits and appearance; male and female look similar. Identified by its dark body, paler head and violet speculum. 21". E.

♀

## Pintail ▶

Seen on lakes and bays, sometimes in huge flocks. Has narrow, pointed wings; flies very swiftly, has dull speculum. Male 27", female 22". B.

Pointed tail

♂

♀

♂

## ◀ American Wigeon

Found on lakes and estuaries; sometimes grazes on land. Has whistling call. Short, stubby bill. Large, white shoulder patches show in flight. 21". B.

9

# Ducks

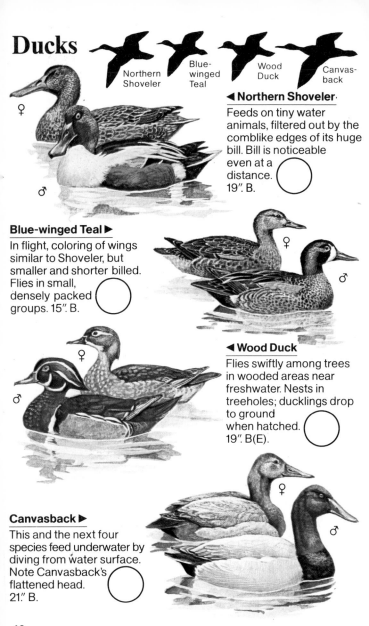

Northern Shoveler

Blue-winged Teal

Wood Duck

Canvas-back

### ◄Northern Shoveler◄

Feeds on tiny water animals, filtered out by the comblike edges of its huge bill. Bill is noticeable even at a distance. 19". B.

### Blue-winged Teal ►

In flight, coloring of wings similar to Shoveler, but smaller and shorter billed. Flies in small, densely packed groups. 15". B.

### ◄ Wood Duck

Flies swiftly among trees in wooded areas near freshwater. Nests in treeholes; ducklings drop to ground when hatched. 19". B(E).

### Canvasback ►

This and the next four species feed underwater by diving from water surface. Note Canvasback's flattened head. 21". B.

Lesser Scaup     Bufflehead     Ruddy Duck     Red-breasted Merganser

# Ducks

## Lesser Scaup ▶

Very similar to **Greater Scaup,** but Lesser has purple- rather than greenish-glossed head and a higher forehead. Seen on salt and freshwater. 17″. B.

## ◀ Bufflehead

Seen on wooded waterways in summer, coasts in winter. Nests in tree hollows or old woodpecker holes. Dives frequently. 14″. B.

## Ruddy Duck ▶

Seen on lakes and ponds; estuaries in winter. Wings are shorter and more rounded than in most ducks. 15″. B.

## ◀ Red-breasted Merganser

Seen by rivers and streams in summer, coasts in winter. Flies with head and neck extended in straight line. 23″. B.

11

# Jaeger, Gulls

### Parasitic Jaeger ▶

Chases other seabirds,
especially terns, across open
sea, forcing them to drop
food, which it then steals.
Sometimes seen
near coasts.
21". B.

Some individual
are dark brown
all over

### ◀ Great Black-backed Gull

Largest of all gulls. Seen
mainly on coastal beaches
and lagoons, rarely on
inland waters. Young are
brown
and white.
30". E.

### Herring Gull ▶

Found on coasts, lakes
and rivers. Often feeds off
garbage dumps. Note pink
feet and black wing-tips
with white
spots.
25". B.

### ◀ Ring-billed Gull

Look for narrow black ring
around bill. Often seen
inland. Young are mottled
brown, tail white with
narrow black
band near tip.
19". B.

### Laughing Gull ▶

Distinguished from other
gulls with black heads by
its all-dark wing-tips. Seen
near coasts. Has a
high, laughing
call.
16". E.

# Terns, Skimmer

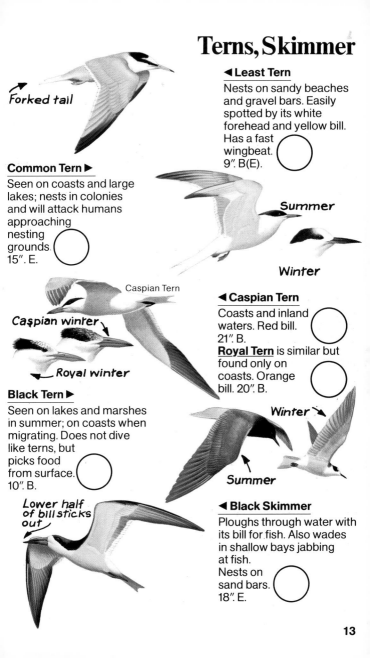

**Forked tail**

### ◄ Least Tern
Nests on sandy beaches and gravel bars. Easily spotted by its white forehead and yellow bill. Has a fast wingbeat. 9″. B(E).

### Common Tern ►
Seen on coasts and large lakes; nests in colonies and will attack humans approaching nesting grounds. 15″. E.

**Summer**

**Winter**

Caspian Tern

**Caspian winter**

**Royal winter**

### ◄ Caspian Tern
Coasts and inland waters. Red bill. 21″. B.
**Royal Tern** is similar but found only on coasts. Orange bill. 20″. B.

### Black Tern ►
Seen on lakes and marshes in summer; on coasts when migrating. Does not dive like terns, but picks food from surface. 10″. B.

**Winter**

**Summer**

**Lower half of bill sticks out**

### ◄ Black Skimmer
Ploughs through water with its bill for fish. Also wades in shallow bays jabbing at fish. Nests on sand bars. 18″. E.

13

# Auks

◀ **Razorbill**
Breeds on cliff ledges
and in crevices. Note
the very deep bill,
flattened at sides.
In winter the
throat is white.
17″. NE.

**Common Murre** ▶
Breeds on rocky ledges;
lays pear shaped egg that
rolls in a circle
not over edge.
17″. B(N).

**Thick-billed Murre**
is very similar.
18″. B(N).

Thick-
billed
Murre

Common Murre

Tufted Puffin

Common Puffin

◀ **Tufted Puffin**
Usually seen on Pacific
sea cliffs. When in flight
watch it use its webbed
feet as brakes.
Nests in burrows.
12″. NW.

◀ **Common Puffin**
Found along Atlantic
coast. Has white
underparts and no
tuft. 12″. NE.

**Cassin's Auklet** ▶
Seen offshore along
Pacific coast, appearing
all dark while swimming
but pale belly is
visible in flight.
7″. W.

# Birds of Prey

Black Vulture

White wing-tips

Short tail

Turkey Vulture

### ◄ Black Vulture
Fast wingbeat.
23″. B(S).

### ◄ Turkey Vulture
Soars in wide circles,
rolling and swaying as it
looks for dead birds and
mammals. Nests in hollow
trees or in rock
crevices.
28″. B.

## Sharp-shinned Hawk ►
A small hawk, with short,
broad wings and a long
tail. Hunts small birds
along woodland edges
and in thickets.
Nests in conifers.
12″. B.

♂

Female larger

Female and young
are brown above
instead of gray

♂

### ◄ Marsh Hawk
Glides low over ground,
its long, rounded wings
allowing it to fly very slowly
as it looks for prey. Nests
on ground in
marshes.
20″. B.

# Birds of Prey

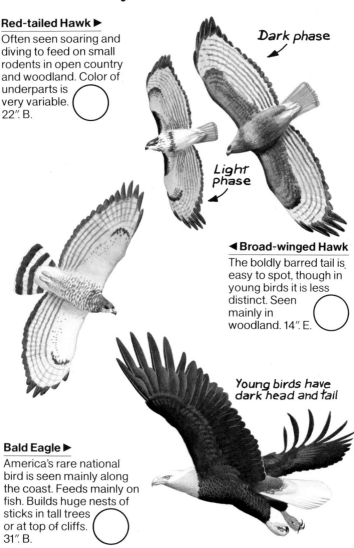

### Red-tailed Hawk ▶

Often seen soaring and diving to feed on small rodents in open country and woodland. Color of underparts is very variable. 22″. B.

*Dark phase*

*Light phase*

### ◀ Broad-winged Hawk

The boldly barred tail is easy to spot, though in young birds it is less distinct. Seen mainly in woodland. 14″. E.

*Young birds have dark head and tail*

### Bald Eagle ▶

America's rare national bird is seen mainly along the coast. Feeds mainly on fish. Builds huge nests of sticks in tall trees or at top of cliffs. 31″. B.

# Birds of Prey, Game Birds

**Osprey ▶**
Large, long winged sea hawk with noticeable bend in wing. Hovers over fish and catches them with talons.
23". B.

*Dark brown line* ↓

*Body is dark brown above* ↗

**◀ American Kestrel**
Seen in countryside and cities, often near highways. Feeds on insects, rodents and small birds. Seeks prey while hovering.
8½". B.

*Rusty tail and back* →

**Turkey ▶**
Wild ancestor of the familiar domestic bird. Seen in open woodland clearings. Male is 48"; female is 36". E(S).

**◀ Spruce Grouse**
Look for the distinctive tail pattern and flanks spotted white. Nests on ground in spruce forests. Cry is a deep hoot.
16". B(N).

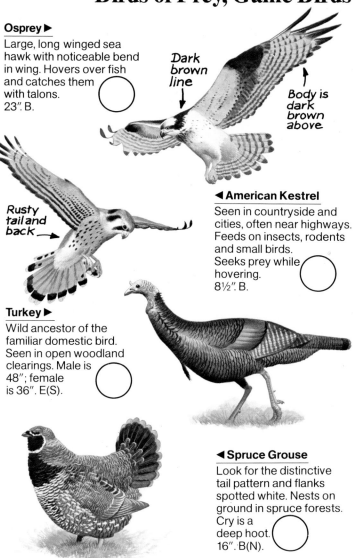

# Game Birds

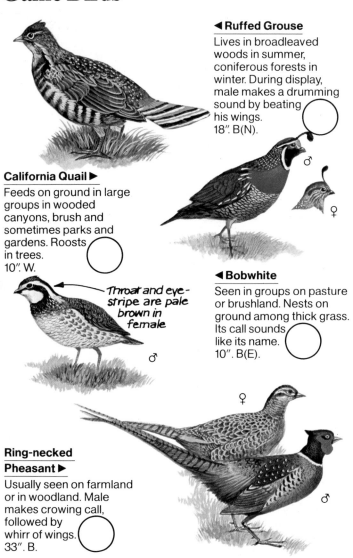

### ◀ Ruffed Grouse
Lives in broadleaved woods in summer, coniferous forests in winter. During display, male makes a drumming sound by beating his wings. 18". B(N).

### California Quail ▶
Feeds on ground in large groups in wooded canyons, brush and sometimes parks and gardens. Roosts in trees. 10". W.

♂

♀

*Throat and eye-stripe are pale brown in female*

♂

### ◀ Bobwhite
Seen in groups on pasture or brushland. Nests on ground among thick grass. Its call sounds like its name. 10". B(E).

♀

♂

### Ring-necked Pheasant ▶
Usually seen on farmland or in woodland. Male makes crowing call, followed by whirr of wings. 33". B.

18

# Crane, Rails

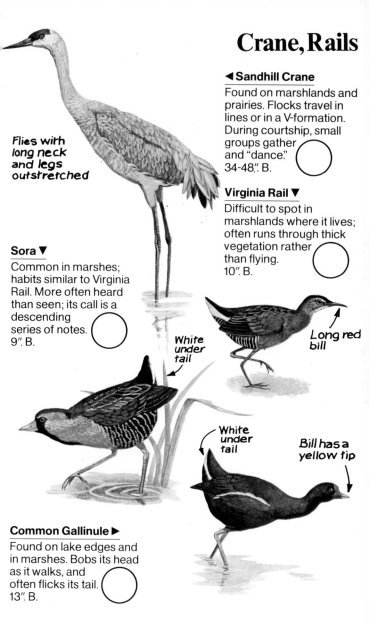

**◄ Sandhill Crane**
Found on marshlands and prairies. Flocks travel in lines or in a V-formation. During courtship, small groups gather and "dance." 34-48". B.

*Flies with long neck and legs outstretched*

**Virginia Rail ▼**
Difficult to spot in marshlands where it lives; often runs through thick vegetation rather than flying. 10". B.

**Sora ▼**
Common in marshes; habits similar to Virginia Rail. More often heard than seen; its call is a descending series of notes. 9". B.

*Long red bill*

*White under tail*

*White under tail*

*Bill has a yellow tip*

**Common Gallinule ►**
Found on lake edges and in marshes. Bobs its head as it walks, and often flicks its tail. 13". B.

# Coot, Shorebirds

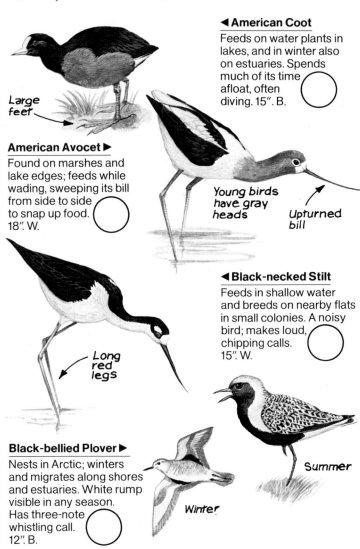

**◄ American Coot**
Feeds on water plants in lakes, and in winter also on estuaries. Spends much of its time afloat, often diving. 15″. B.

*Large feet*

**American Avocet ►**
Found on marshes and lake edges; feeds while wading, sweeping its bill from side to side to snap up food. 18″. W.

*Young birds have gray heads*

*Upturned bill*

**◄ Black-necked Stilt**
Feeds in shallow water and breeds on nearby flats in small colonies. A noisy bird; makes loud, chipping calls. 15″. W.

*Long red legs*

**Black-bellied Plover ►**
Nests in Arctic; winters and migrates along shores and estuaries. White rump visible in any season. Has three-note whistling call. 12″. B.

*Winter*

*Summer*

20

# Shorebirds

### Semipalmated Plover ▶
Found on sandy or muddy shores. Nests in a scrape on beaches. Young have brown head and breast markings. Has a two-note call. 7". B.

*White wing bar shows in flight*

*Often bobs its head*

### ◀ Killdeer
Often seen far from water in fields, airports and even by highways. Pretends to be injured if its nest is approached. Tail shows in flight. 10". B.

### Whimbrel ▶
Seen on marshes, prairies and shores. The call is a series of rapid whistles. 17". B.

*Black tip*

### ◀ Marbled Godwit
Long, slightly upturned bill. Rusty wing linings show in flight. Breeds on prairies, winters on coast. Makes shallow grass nest. 18". B(W).

# Shorebirds

*Walks with a constant bobbing motion*

**◀ Spotted Sandpiper**

Breeds near streams and lakes; winters on coasts. Flies with shallow, flicking wing beat; white wing bar shows in flight. 7½″. B.

**Willet ▶**

A stoutly built sandpiper, seen near lakes and salt marshes. One of its calls sounds like its name. Chest is mottled brown in spring. 15″. B(W).

*Striking wing pattern shows in flight*

**◀ Greater Yellowlegs**

Winters on salt marshes. Loud calls are given in threes or fours. Slim build, bright yellow legs. 14″. B.

**Short-billed Dowitcher ▶**

Seen mainly on mud shores and salt marshes. Has a long bill. 12″. B(E).

*Winter*

*Summer*

# Shorebirds

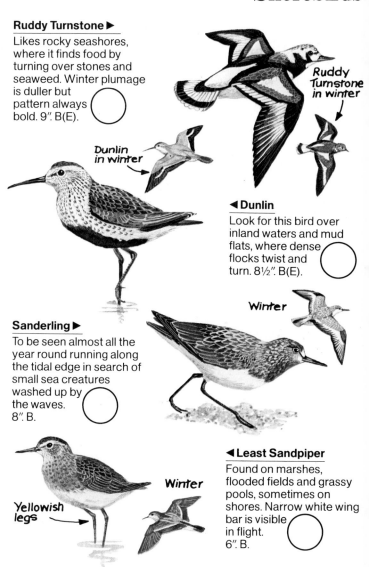

### Ruddy Turnstone ▶
Likes rocky seashores, where it finds food by turning over stones and seaweed. Winter plumage is duller but pattern always bold. 9″. B(E).

Ruddy Turnstone in winter

Dunlin in winter

### ◀ Dunlin
Look for this bird over inland waters and mud flats, where dense flocks twist and turn. 8½″. B(E).

Winter

### Sanderling ▶
To be seen almost all the year round running along the tidal edge in search of small sea creatures washed up by the waves. 8″. B.

### ◀ Least Sandpiper
Found on marshes, flooded fields and grassy pools, sometimes on shores. Narrow white wing bar is visible in flight. 6″. B.

Winter

Yellowish legs

# Shorebirds, Woodcock, Snipe

Has stouter bill than Least Sandpiper

Black legs

Winter→

◄**Semipalmated Sandpiper**
Seen mainly on shore or at river and lake edges; forms large flocks on migration. Its feet are partly webbed.
6½". E.

Notice wing stripe

**Northern Phalarope ►**
Swims floating high on water, sometimes spinning to disturb prey. Breeds near inland pools but winters at sea.
7". B(W).

Summer
♀

Plumage looks like leaves

◄**American Woodcock**
Active mainly at night. Difficult to see in damp woodlands where it lives because of its good camouflage coloring. 11". E.

**Common Snipe ►**
Prefers swampland, pools and ditches. When disturbed, rises with harsh call and flies away in zigzags. Nests in damp meadows, marshes. 11". B.

24

# Pigeon, Doves, Cuckoos

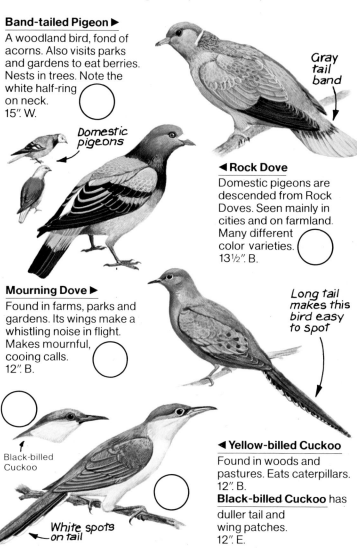

### Band-tailed Pigeon ▶
A woodland bird, fond of acorns. Also visits parks and gardens to eat berries. Nests in trees. Note the white half-ring on neck.
15″. W.

Gray tail band

Domestic pigeons

### ◀ Rock Dove
Domestic pigeons are descended from Rock Doves. Seen mainly in cities and on farmland. Many different color varieties.
13½″. B.

### Mourning Dove ▶
Found in farms, parks and gardens. Its wings make a whistling noise in flight. Makes mournful, cooing calls.
12″. B.

Long tail makes this bird easy to spot

Black-billed Cuckoo

White spots on tail

### ◀ Yellow-billed Cuckoo
Found in woods and pastures. Eats caterpillars.
12″. B.
**Black-billed Cuckoo** has duller tail and wing patches.
12″. E.

25

# Roadrunner, Owls

### Roadrunner ▶
Large ground living
cuckoo of deserts and dry
bushland. Runs rapidly
after prey such as
lizards and
snakes.
22″. W.

Bushy
crest

Gray phase

Red phase

### ◀ Screech Owl
Found in woods, gardens
and orchards. Nests in tree
hollows. May attack
humans who come too
near. Gray, brown and
reddish color phases
(varieties)
occur.
10″. B.

### Great Horned Owl ▶
Found in all types of
habitat, including parks
and gardens. Nests on
cliff ledges or in old nests
of hawks
or crows.
25″. B.

# Owls, Whip-poor-will, Nighthawk

### Barred Owl ▶

Found in damp woods and swamp forests. Roosts in tree foliage and comes out at night to seek prey. Usually nests in tree hollows. 20″. E.

Dark eyes

### Whip-poor-will ▶

Found on woodland edges. Almost invisible on ground because of camouflaged plumage. Active at night; catches insects in flight. 10″. E(&SW).

### ◀ Saw-whet Owl

Found in conifers and other evergreens. Very tame if approached at roosting place in daylight. Eats small rodents. 7″. B.

Wings more pointed than Whip-poor-will's

### ◀ Common Nighthawk

Found in cities and open country. Active mostly in early evening; also seen in daytime and at night. Often nests on roofs. 10″. B.

# Swift, Hummingbirds

Short tail →

◄ **Chimney Swift**
Always on the wing, except when at nest on wall of cave or chimney. Narrower wings than Swallow. 5½". E

### Ruby-throated
### Hummingbird ►
Hovers over flowers to feed on nectar. Wings beat so fast they are invisible and make a humming sound. 3½". E.

Male has red throat

♂

♀

◄ **Black-chinned**
**Hummingbird**
Found in many habitats; will visit special hummingbird feeders in gardens. 3½". W.

♂

Female has white throat

### Rufous Hummingbird ►
Found in many habitats, including woodlands. Female is less brightly colored than male. Builds a tiny nest on tree branch. 4". W.

Female has black and white tail

♂

28

# Kingfisher, Woodpeckers

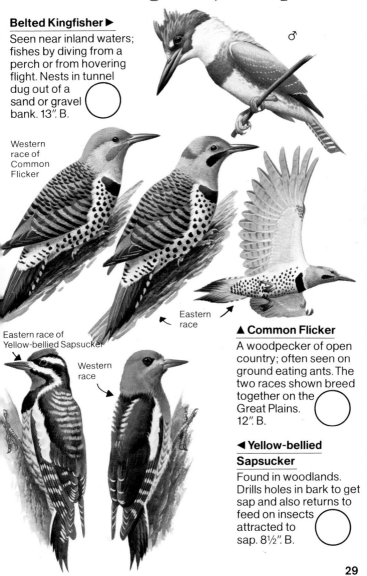

**Belted Kingfisher ►**

Seen near inland waters; fishes by diving from a perch or from hovering flight. Nests in tunnel dug out of a sand or gravel bank. 13″. B.

♂

Western race of Common Flicker

Eastern race

Eastern race of Yellow-bellied Sapsucker

Western race

**▲ Common Flicker**

A woodpecker of open country; often seen on ground eating ants. The two races shown breed together on the Great Plains. 12″. B.

**◄ Yellow-bellied Sapsucker**

Found in woodlands. Drills holes in bark to get sap and also returns to feed on insects attracted to sap. 8½″. B.

# Woodpeckers, Flycatchers

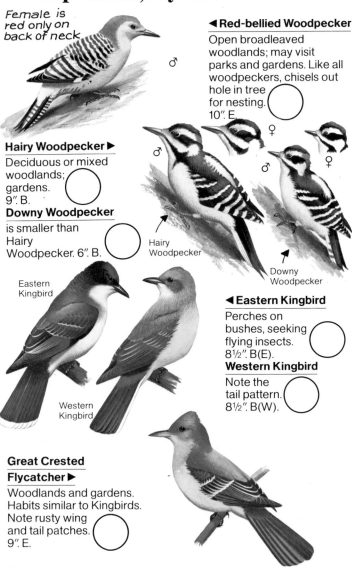

*Female is red only on back of neck*

♂

### ◄ Red-bellied Woodpecker

Open broadleaved woodlands; may visit parks and gardens. Like all woodpeckers, chisels out hole in tree for nesting. 10″. E.

♀

### Hairy Woodpecker ►

Deciduous or mixed woodlands; gardens. 9″. B.

### Downy Woodpecker

is smaller than Hairy Woodpecker. 6″. B.

♂

♂

♀

Hairy Woodpecker

Downy Woodpecker

Eastern Kingbird

### ◄ Eastern Kingbird

Perches on bushes, seeking flying insects. 8½″. B(E).

### Western Kingbird

Note the tail pattern. 8½″. B(W).

Western Kingbird

### Great Crested Flycatcher ►

Woodlands and gardens. Habits similar to Kingbirds. Note rusty wing and tail patches. 9″. E.

### Eastern Phoebe ▶

Usually seen near nesting places on cliffs or bridges and around farm buildings. Wags its tail continually. Sometimes stays through winter. 7". E.

### ◀ Alder Flycatcher and Willow Flycatcher

Two species of almost exactly the same color and shape. Both like to hunt insects in thickets. 6". B.

### Eastern Wood Pewee ▶

Found in woodland, often high up, where it is difficult to see, but its call ("pee-o-wee") can be heard. 6½". E.

### ◀ Horned Lark

Found on open ground and seashores. Rarely perches; moves on ground by walking, not hopping. Forms large flocks in winter. 7½". B.

# Swallows

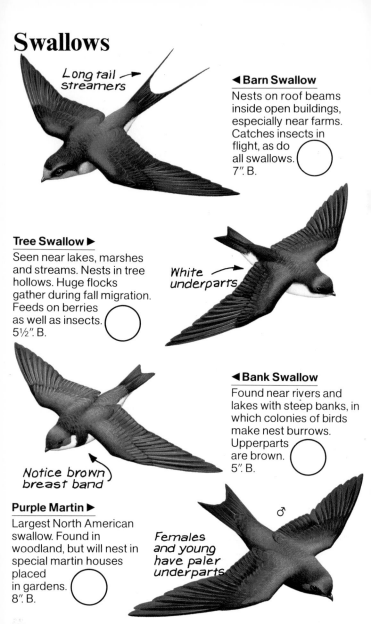

Long tail streamers

**◄ Barn Swallow**
Nests on roof beams inside open buildings, especially near farms. Catches insects in flight, as do all swallows. 7″. B.

**Tree Swallow ►**
Seen near lakes, marshes and streams. Nests in tree hollows. Huge flocks gather during fall migration. Feeds on berries as well as insects. 5½″. B.

White underparts

**◄ Bank Swallow**
Found near rivers and lakes with steep banks, in which colonies of birds make nest burrows. Upperparts are brown. 5″. B.

Notice brown breast band

**Purple Martin ►**
Largest North American swallow. Found in woodland, but will nest in special martin houses placed in gardens. 8″. B.

♂

Females and young have paler underparts

# Jays, Magpies

### ◄ Blue Jay

Found in deciduous and mixed woods; parks, gardens and backyards in suburbs. Fond of oak trees. Builds a stick nest in the fork of a tree. 12″. E.

### Steller's Jay ►

Prefers conifers and mixed woods for nesting. Moves to oak woods in winter. Like the Blue Jay, imitates Hawks. 13″. W.

Yellow-billed Magpie

Black-billed Magpie

### ◄ Black-billed Magpie

Prefers open country with bushes in which it makes large domed nest. 20″. B.

### Yellow-billed Magpie

nests in colonies. 17″. W.

# Raven, Crow, Chickadee, Titmouse

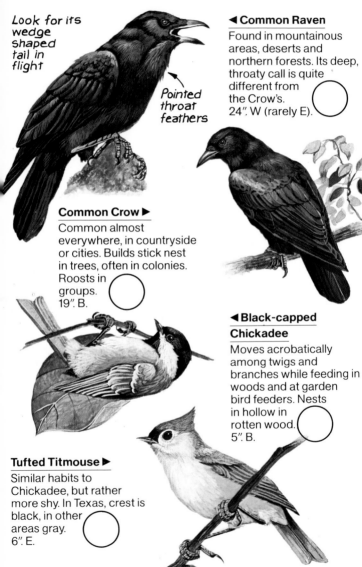

Look for its wedge shaped tail in flight

Pointed throat feathers

### ◄ Common Raven
Found in mountainous areas, deserts and northern forests. Its deep, throaty call is quite different from the Crow's. 24". W (rarely E).

### Common Crow ►
Common almost everywhere, in countryside or cities. Builds stick nest in trees, often in colonies. Roosts in groups. 19". B.

### ◄ Black-capped Chickadee
Moves acrobatically among twigs and branches while feeding in woods and at garden bird feeders. Nests in hollow in rotten wood. 5". B.

### Tufted Titmouse ►
Similar habits to Chickadee, but rather more shy. In Texas, crest is black, in other areas gray. 6". E.

# Dipper, Nuthatches, Creeper

### Dipper ▶

Looks like a giant wren. Found by swift-flowing rivers; often perches on rock, bobbing. Moves with ease underwater to find food. 8". W.

### ◀ White-breasted Nuthatch

Seen in broadleaved woods, climbing trees to find food in bark. Nests in tree holes. Visits bird feeders. 5½". B.

### Red-breasted Nuthatch ▶

Seen in coniferous woods. Habits similar to White-breasted, but visits gardens less and is shyer. 4½". B.

*Climbs downward head first*

### ◀ Brown Creeper

Like Nuthatches, feeds from bark, but usually climbs upward, supporting itself on stiff tail feathers. Nests behind loose bark or in ivy. 5½". B.

# Wrens, Mockingbird

### ◀ House Wren
Seen in woods, farmland, suburbs, usually in bushes. Uses nest boxes, sometimes getting rid of birds nesting there by destroying their eggs. 5". B.

*Often cocks tail upward*

*Wide tail has white tip*

### Bewick's Wren ▶
Found on farmland, in shrubs and thickets. Has loud, bubbling song. Often jerks tail sideways, as well as cocking it up. 5½". B(W).

### ◀ Long-billed Marsh Wren
Common among reeds and cattails on marshes, where it weaves its nest around reeds. 5". B.

### Mockingbird ▶
Found in country, parks, suburbs. Famous for its songs, which include imitations of other birds. Jerks tail from side to side. 10". B.

*White wing patches show in flight*

# Mockingbirds, Robin, Thrush

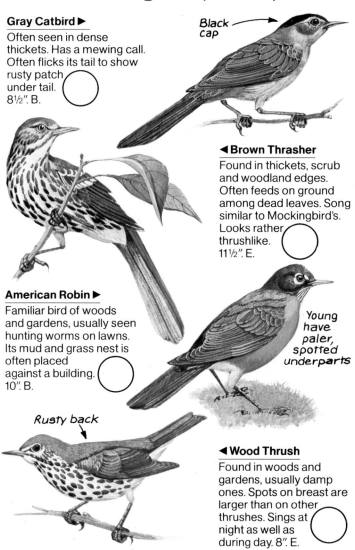

### Gray Catbird ▶
Often seen in dense thickets. Has a mewing call. Often flicks its tail to show rusty patch under tail. 8½". B.

Black cap

### ◀ Brown Thrasher
Found in thickets, scrub and woodland edges. Often feeds on ground among dead leaves. Song similar to Mockingbird's. Looks rather thrushlike. 11½". E.

### American Robin ▶
Familiar bird of woods and gardens, usually seen hunting worms on lawns. Its mud and grass nest is often placed against a building. 10". B.

Young have paler, spotted underparts

Rusty back

### ◀ Wood Thrush
Found in woods and gardens, usually damp ones. Spots on breast are larger than on other thrushes. Sings at night as well as during day. 8". E.

# Thrushes, Kinglet

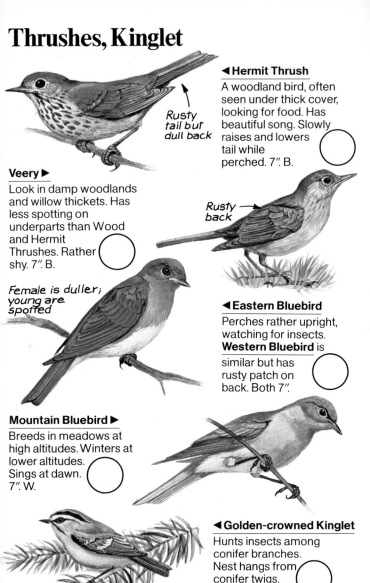

Rusty tail but dull back

### ◀ Hermit Thrush
A woodland bird, often seen under thick cover, looking for food. Has beautiful song. Slowly raises and lowers tail while perched. 7". B.

### Veery ▶
Look in damp woodlands and willow thickets. Has less spotting on underparts than Wood and Hermit Thrushes. Rather shy. 7". B.

*Female is duller; young are spotted*

Rusty back

### ◀ Eastern Bluebird
Perches rather upright, watching for insects. **Western Bluebird** is similar but has rusty patch on back. Both 7".

### Mountain Bluebird ▶
Breeds in meadows at high altitudes. Winters at lower altitudes. Sings at dawn. 7". W.

### ◀ Golden-crowned Kinglet
Hunts insects among conifer branches. Nest hangs from conifer twigs. 4". B.

# Waxwing, Starling, Vireos

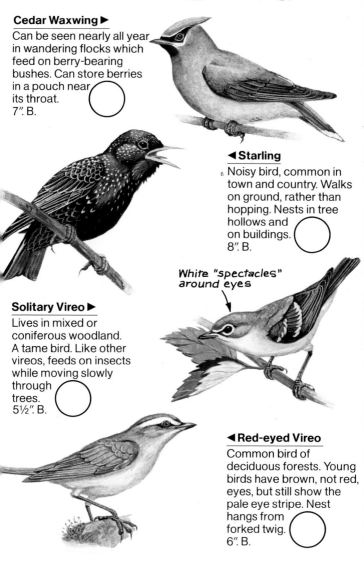

### Cedar Waxwing ▶
Can be seen nearly all year in wandering flocks which feed on berry-bearing bushes. Can store berries in a pouch near its throat.
7". B.

### ◀ Starling
Noisy bird, common in town and country. Walks on ground, rather than hopping. Nests in tree hollows and on buildings.
8". B.

White "spectacles" around eyes

### Solitary Vireo ▶
Lives in mixed or coniferous woodland. A tame bird. Like other vireos, feeds on insects while moving slowly through trees.
5½". B.

### ◀ Red-eyed Vireo
Common bird of deciduous forests. Young birds have brown, not red, eyes, but still show the pale eye stripe. Nest hangs from forked twig.
6". B.

# Warblers

The warblers on these pages are shown in their spring plumage. In fall, their plumage changes and makes them more difficult to identify.

### ◄ Black-and-white Warbler

Creeps along tree trunks looking for food, rather like Nuthatch. Seen mainly in deciduous woods; in gardens and parks on migration. 5". B.

### Yellow-rumped Warbler ►

Seen in spruce forests, and on coasts during migration. Western birds have yellow throats; Eastern birds have white throats. Nests in conifers. 5½". B.

Eastern race

### ◄ Northern Parula

Found in woodland, often near swamps; prefers conifers. Builds its nest inside tufts of spanish moss or lichens on tree limbs. 4½". E.

### Yellow Warbler ►

Look in willow thickets, orchards and gardens. Cup shaped nest is placed in the fork of a sapling. Has yellow spots on tail. 5". B.

# Warblers

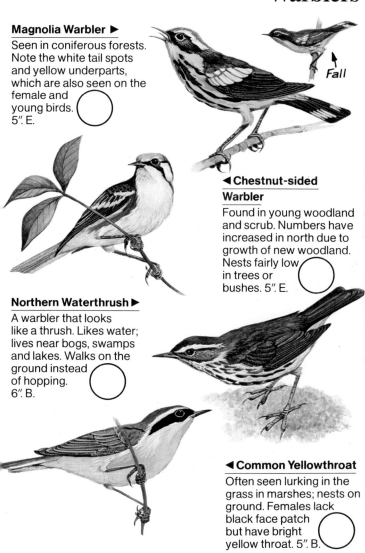

**Magnolia Warbler ▶**
Seen in coniferous forests.
Note the white tail spots
and yellow underparts,
which are also seen on the
female and
young birds.
5″. E.

Fall

**◀ Chestnut-sided
Warbler**
Found in young woodland
and scrub. Numbers have
increased in north due to
growth of new woodland.
Nests fairly low
in trees or
bushes. 5″. E.

**Northern Waterthrush ▶**
A warbler that looks
like a thrush. Likes water;
lives near bogs, swamps
and lakes. Walks on the
ground instead
of hopping.
6″. B.

**◀ Common Yellowthroat**
Often seen lurking in the
grass in marshes; nests on
ground. Females lack
black face patch
but have bright
yellow throat. 5″. B.

# Warblers, Blackbirds

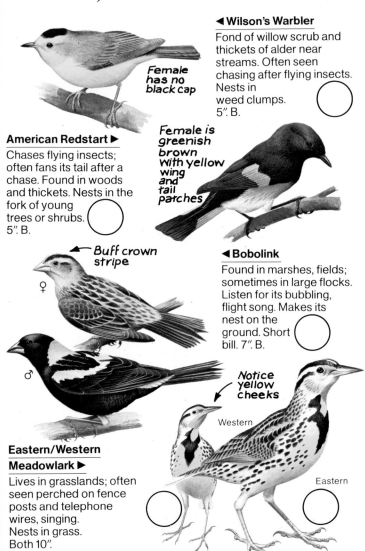

### ◄ Wilson's Warbler
Fond of willow scrub and thickets of alder near streams. Often seen chasing after flying insects. Nests in weed clumps. 5". B.

*Female has no black cap*

### American Redstart ►
Chases flying insects; often fans its tail after a chase. Found in woods and thickets. Nests in the fork of young trees or shrubs. 5". B.

*Female is greenish brown with yellow wing and tail patches*

*Buff crown stripe*

♀

### ◄ Bobolink
Found in marshes, fields; sometimes in large flocks. Listen for its bubbling, flight song. Makes its nest on the ground. Short bill. 7". B.

♂

*Notice yellow cheeks*

Western

Eastern

### Eastern/Western Meadowlark ►
Lives in grasslands; often seen perched on fence posts and telephone wires, singing. Nests in grass. Both 10".

# Blackbirds, Oriole

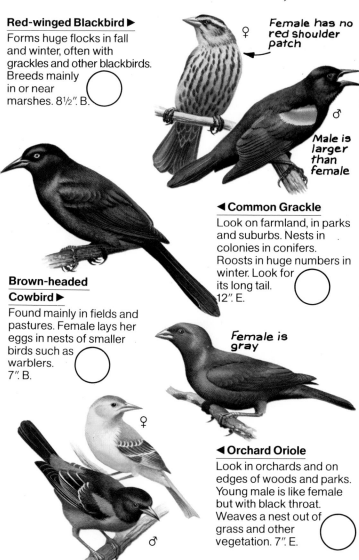

### Red-winged Blackbird ►
Forms huge flocks in fall and winter, often with grackles and other blackbirds. Breeds mainly in or near marshes. 8½". B.

♀ Female has no red shoulder patch

♂

Male is larger than female

### ◄ Common Grackle
Look on farmland, in parks and suburbs. Nests in colonies in conifers. Roosts in huge numbers in winter. Look for its long tail. 12". E.

### Brown-headed Cowbird ►
Found mainly in fields and pastures. Female lays her eggs in nests of smaller birds such as warblers. 7". B.

Female is gray

♀

### ◄ Orchard Oriole
Look in orchards and on edges of woods and parks. Young male is like female but with black throat. Weaves a nest out of grass and other vegetation. 7". E.

♂

# Orioles, Tanagers, Cardinal

**◄ Northern Oriole**
Likes tall trees in woods or city parks; builds basketlike nest which hangs from tips of branches. 8″. B.

♀
♂
Eastern race
Western race

**Western Tanager ►**
Feeds high in trees, usually conifers or oaks, making it difficult to see. Nests in pine or oak branch; lays 3-4 speckled eggs. 7″. W.

♂
♀

**◄ Scarlet Tanager**
Found in woods, often high up in trees. Note male's all-black wings. Male may be patched with green when molting in fall. 7½″. E.

♂

*Breeding plumage*

♀

Crest

**Cardinal ►**
Common garden bird, also seen in thickets and edges of woods. Both male and female can be heard singing throughout the year. 8½″. E(&SW).

♂

# Grosbeaks, Buntings, Finch

### Rose-breasted Grosbeak ▶
Found in woods, orchards and gardens. Male has rosy patch under wing which shows in flight. Nest is placed on a low branch. 8″. E.

♂   ♀

Yellow underwings show in flight

### ◀ Evening Grosbeak
Nests in conifers. May be seen at garden feeders in winter; is very fond of sunflower seeds. Notice its very large bill. 8″. B.

♂   ♀

### Indigo Bunting ▶
Seen in hedges and near woods. Nests in bushes. 5½″. E.

### Lazuli Bunting ▶
Male often sings from a tree or telephone wire. 5½″. W.

Lazuli Bunting

Indigo Bunting

♀   ♂

### ◀ House Finch
Found in brush, desert, orchards and suburbs in West; cities, particularly New York, in East. Nests in bushes or on buildings. 5½″. B(W).

♂   ♀

# Finches, Dickcissel, Towhee

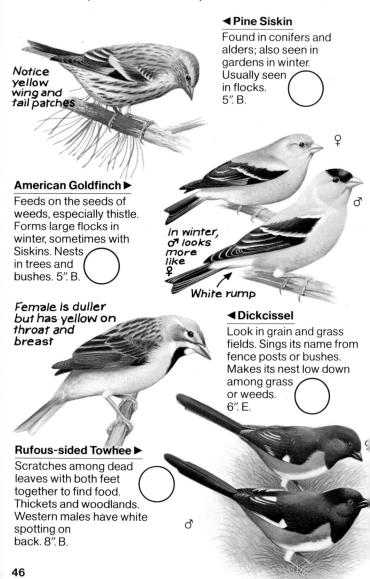

**◄ Pine Siskin**
Found in conifers and alders; also seen in gardens in winter. Usually seen in flocks. 5". B.

*Notice yellow wing and tail patches*

**American Goldfinch ►**
Feeds on the seeds of weeds, especially thistle. Forms large flocks in winter, sometimes with Siskins. Nests in trees and bushes. 5". B.

♀

*In winter, ♂ looks more like ♀*

White rump

*Female is duller but has yellow on throat and breast*

**◄ Dickcissel**
Look in grain and grass fields. Sings its name from fence posts or bushes. Makes its nest low down among grass or weeds. 6". E.

**Rufous-sided Towhee ►**
Scratches among dead leaves with both feet together to find food. Thickets and woodlands. Western males have white spotting on back. 8". B.

♂

# Junco, Sparrows

### Dark-eyed Junco ▶
Seen in coniferous forests in summer; visits fields and gardens in winter. Western "Oregon" race (not shown) has black hood, chestnut back. 6". B.

Eastern "slate-colored" race

*Female has no black "bib"*

♂

### ◀ House Sparrow
European bird, introduced to New York in 1850; now very common in cities and farmland throughout North America. Not a true sparrow. Untidy nest. 6". B.

### Tree Sparrow ▶
Breeds in far north; in winter visits willow and birch scrub, fields and thickets. Can be seen in flocks, making "tinkling" sound. 6". B.

*Notice dark spot on breast*

### ◀ Chipping Sparrow
Common in gardens and parks, where it often feeds on lawns. Nests in dense shrubbery and lines its nest with animal hair. 5½". B.

# Sparrows

*Tends to sit more upright than White-throated Sparrow*

## White-throated Sparrow ▶

Breeds in conifer woods; winters in scrub and gardens. Feeds on ground. Nests on or near ground. Winter flocks roost in thickets. 6½". B.

## ◀ White-crowned Sparrow

Similar to White-throated Sparrow but has thinner body and no white throat. Visits woods and gardens in winter. Nests in low shrubbery. 7". B.

*White throat*

*Eastern race has fox-red stripes and spots*

Western race

## ◀ Fox Sparrow

Scratches for food among dead leaves like Towhee (see p. 46). Found in conifer woods in summer; thickets and rough pasture in winter. 7". B.

## Song Sparrow ▶

Look in thickets, bushes and also in parks. Size varies and color ranges from pale to dark brown. Wags its tail as it flies. 6". B.

*Young birds don't have this spot*

# Hints on birdwatching

Why watch birds? Birds are everywhere at all seasons of the year, which makes watching them a good hobby. It is easy to start – just look out your window. No great skill or knowledge is needed and there is no limit to what you can learn. You probably already know some birds: Robin, Jay, Pigeon, Crow, House Sparrow, Starling, Swallow and Cardinal.

Wherever you live you can see birds all year. But you will see the greatest number and variety of birds during the spring and fall. This is when the birds migrate; that is, they move from one place to another. Depending on where you live, spring migration can start as early as March and end as late as May; fall migration starts, some places, as early as the end of August and goes on until November. Some birds migrate early, others later; still others (like the Cardinal) do not migrate at all.

## Identifying birds

The best way to start birdwatching is to learn to identify the birds you see. When out birding, keep your binoculars handy. Learn to focus them quickly, while keeping your eye on the bird.

Ask yourself these questions when you see a bird:

*Where* did you see it? Where the bird is found (its *habitat*) is one step in identification. Birds may be grouped according to where they live: herons are found on beaches or in marshes; Bobwhites in fields; and warblers in trees or bushes. You won't see a Pheasant in the water or a Canada Goose on a tree.

Then notice the *way it flies.* Does it fly in a straight line? Does it glide, bounce or hover?

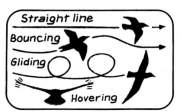

Next look at the *color* of the bird's feathers. Are there any special *markings,* such as wingbars, collars or eye stripes? Is the *breast* white, spotted, streaked, or barred?

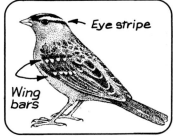

What *shape* is the bird, and what shape is its tail? How does the bird *swim, perch* or *stand*? What is the bird's *size*? Is it as big as a Crow? a Robin? a Sparrow?

Different birds have different *songs or calls.* Song is another means of identifying birds, but this is difficult, and songs are hard to describe. There are a few songs, though, that are easy. These songs are the name of the bird, like To-whee and Bob-white. Birds use song in courtship and also to defend their nesting territory.

## Nests

Birds' nests are made of a great variety of materials and are found in many places: on sand dunes (Black Skimmers), on cliffs (Razorbills), under overhangs or eaves (Barn Swallows), and in holes in trees. Some birds are called colonial birds. They nest very close together (egrets, herons, and terns). Some birds make no nests at all (Whip-poor-wills).

Most small birds, like warblers, and finches, build small cuplike nests. They use grasses and sometimes animal hair.

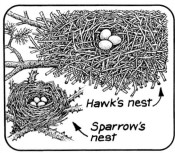

Hawk's nest

Sparrow's nest

Larger birds, like hawks and owls, build their nests with large sticks. Sometimes they use an old nest. With experience, you will be able to identify birds' nests, too. If you get too close to a bird's nest you might harm the bird. That is not what you mean to do, but it is often the result. Some birds will chase you away; terns and gulls will dive at you. But others may get frightened and leave the nest. So it is *very* important *never* to approach a nest too closely or to touch the bird's eggs. For birds that nest on the ground the danger is even greater – you might step in the nest by mistake. It is *illegal* to disturb nesting birds or their eggs. The best thing to do is to leave nesting birds alone. Birdwatch from a distance; use your binoculars.

## Fascinating facts

Even though there seems to be a lot to look for in birding, don't get discouraged because it is really very easy. And birds are fascinating creatures. They change their feathers (molt) every year. Some birds, like goldfinches, have special feathers for the breeding season only. Owls have such terrific hearing that they hear their prey rather than see it – after all, they hunt at night. And Arctic Terns fly around the globe, from Alaska to Antarctica every year. Wading birds have webbed feet so they can walk on marshy ground, while perching birds (like finches) have feet that lock around a branch or wire to keep them from falling off (see picture).

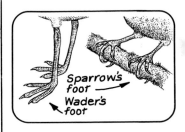

Sparrow's foot

Wader's foot

## Things to remember

There are a few things to be careful about when you go birdwatching. It is not a good idea to go off by yourself unless you know the area you are hiking. There is a chance of hurting your feet in rocky country, of spraining your ankle in a boggy marsh, or of getting lost in the woods. Learn to recognize poison ivy and poison oak. Be aware of snakes and other wildlife in the area where you are walking. Remember: it is their home – you are a visitor.

# Identifying shapes

One of the ways you can learn to recognize different birds is by their shape, which is often very distinctive. See if you can identify the birds shown on this page. The answers are below.

1. Mallard 2. Loon 3. Red-tailed Hawk
4. Bobwhite 5. Snowy Egret 6. Belted Kingfisher
7. Herring Gull 8. Common Flicker
9. Mockingbird 10. Barn Swallow
11. American Robin 12. Cardinal 13. Starling
14. White-breasted Nuthatch

# Making a bird table feeder

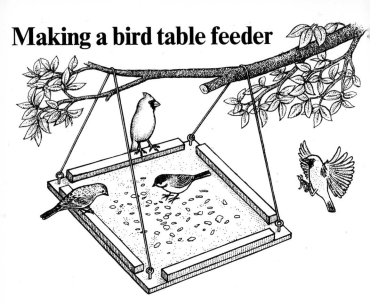

Why not make a bird table feeder for your backyard or windowsill? This is a good way to attract birds and you will be helping them to survive the winter.

Suitable foods are sunflower seeds, thistle seeds, birdseed mixtures (sold in most supermarkets), breadcrumbs, cracked corn, peanuts, raisins, apples and suet (beef fat).

Feed the birds every day from October to April. There should be enough natural food for them in the summer, though some people feed the birds all year round. If you put out food for the birds, do it every day. Do not stop suddenly, especially if the weather is cold, because the birds will be counting on you for their food. It is also important to keep the bird table clean.

These pictures show you how to make a simple bird table feeder.

**You will need:**
1. A piece of ¾"-thick plywood, 18" square.
2. 4 strips of softwood (like pine), 1" x 1", 14" long.
3. 8 screws and a screwdriver.
4. Glue.
5. A wood preservative (stain or varnish) and a paintbrush.
6. Nylon string.
7. 4 screw eyes.

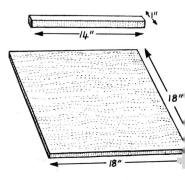

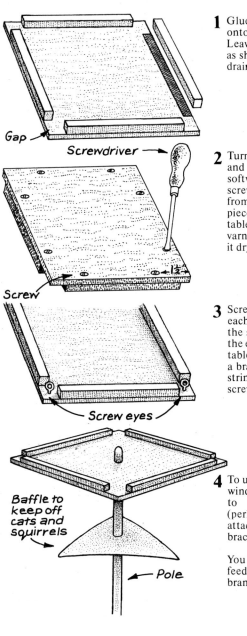

**1** Glue the softwood strips onto the plywood square. Leave gaps at each corner, as shown, to let rainwater drain off.

Gap

Screwdriver

**2** Turn the plywood over, and screw the pieces of softwood down. Use two screws (on each side), 1½" from the end of each piece. Paint the whole table (both sides) with varnish or stain and let it dry for at least 24 hours.

Screw

**3** Screw one screw eye into each corner as shown. Tie the string tightly through the eyes on one side of the table. Hang the table over a branch and then tie the string to the other two screw eyes.

Screw eyes

Baffle to keep off cats and squirrels

Pole

**4** To use this feeder on your windowsill, you may have to make it narrower (perhaps 18" x 9") and attach it to a pair of brackets.

You can also put this feeder up on a pole if a branch is not handy.

# Making a suet feeder

Insect-eating birds, such as woodpeckers, prefer suet to seed. Other birds, too, need suet to supplement their diet. If you have a suet feeder in addition to a bird table, you will attract a wide variety of birds to your yard. You can get suet from your butcher or from the meat counter at your supermarket.

Fill your suet feeder regularly. You can make or buy suet seed cakes, or just stuff chunks of plain suet into the feeder.

Here is how to make a simple suet feeder that will attach to a tree trunk.

**You will need:**
1. A piece of ¾"-thick plywood, 8" x 4".
2. A wood preservative (stain or varnish) and a paintbrush.
3. A piece of wire mesh, 8" square, with ½" openings.
4. 9 staple nails and a hammer.
5. A screw eye and a 1½"-long nail.

**1**

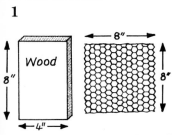

Stain or varnish the wood on all sides. Let it dry for 24 hours.

**2**

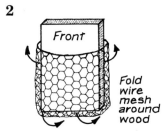

Bend the mesh around the wood to form a type of envelope or thin basket. The wire should be about 1" away from the wood.

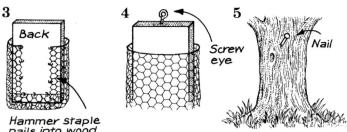

**3**

Turn the wood over and nail down the mesh, using the staple nails. Use three nails on each side.

**4**

Screw the screw eye onto the top of the feeder.

**5**

Hammer the 1½" nail into a tree trunk, at a slight angle. Hang your feeder.

# Backyard bird survey

Why not keep a record of the birds that visit your yard? The more feeders and different types of food you have, the more species of birds you'll attract. It is good to know what certain birds like to eat. Here is a list of some birds and the foods they like.

| Birds | Food |
|---|---|
| Cardinal, Pine Siskin, Junco, Titmouse, Nuthatches, Finches, Chickadee, Grosbeaks, Jays, Sparrows, Doves, Crossbills | Sunflower seed |
| Pheasant, Chickadee, Cardinal, Titmouse, Jays, Doves | Cracked corn |
| Goldfinch, Chickadee, Pine Siskin | Thistle seed |
| Mockingbird, Catbird | Raisins |
| Robin, Mockingbird, Wrens | Apple pieces |
| Woodpeckers, Wrens, Chickadee, Nuthatches, Starling, Finches, Brown Creeper, Titmouse | Suet |

It is also very important to have water for the birds. A simple birdbath (not too deep) will do. Put it in a sunny spot. Because birds have no teeth, they need to eat grit. The grit helps them to digest (grind up) their food. If you have a bird table, you might set one corner aside for grit. Birds also like the berries of certain trees and shrubs.

The chart below is an example of a backyard survey. Perhaps you'd like to keep one like this.

| NAMES OF BIRDS SEEN | MONTH WHEN SEEN J F M A M J J A S O N D | FOODS EATEN | BATHE | DRINK | WHERE THEY NEST |
|---|---|---|---|---|---|
| Chickadee | ✓✓✓✓✓✓✓✓✓✓✓ | Suet, sunflower seed | ✓ | ✓ | In bird house. |
| Robin | ✓✓✓✓✓✓✓ | worms | | ✓ | Don't know. |
| Red-winged Blackbird | ✓✓ ✓✓ | Mixed bird seed | ✓ | ✓ | Don't know. |
| House sparrow | ✓✓✓✓✓✓✓✓✓ | Mixed seed, sunflower seed | ✓ | ✓ | Under porch eaves. |

# Organizations you can join

As a birdwatcher, you may want to join a conservation or birding society. Many of them sponsor trips and educational or interpretive programs. Some maintain sanctuaries and nature centers. A few of the major North American organizations are listed here:

American Birding Association, Box 4335, Austin, TX 78765.
*National Audubon Society, 950 Third Avenue, New York, NY 10022.
National Wildlife Federation, 1412 16 Street NW, Washington, DC 20036.
*The Nature Conservancy, National Office, 1800 N. Kent Street, Arlington, VA 22209.

*Sierra Club, National Office, 1050 Mills Tower, San Fransisco, CA 94104.
Canadian Nature Federation, 46 Elgin Street, Ottawa, Ontario K1P 5K6.
Long Point Bird Observatory, Box 160, Port Rowan, Ontario NOE 1MO.

*These organizations have local chapters. There may be one where you live. To find out, write them at the above address or ask at your public library. In addition, there might be a local bird club or nature group that you could join.

# Books to read

*Birds of North America; a Guide to Field Identification.* Robbins, Bruun, and Zim (Golden/ paperback). Uses color pictures and range maps.
*A Field Guide to Birds.* Roger Tory Peterson (Houghton Mifflin/ paperback). In two volumes, eastern and western. Most pictures in color. There is a special guide for Texas and nearby states.
*The Audubon Society Field Guide to North American Birds.* (Knopf). In two volumes, eastern and western. Has color photos.
*Watching Birds; an Introduction to Ornithology.* Roger Tory Peterson (Houghton Mifflin).
*The Birdwatcher's Bible.* George Laycock (Doubleday/ paperback). Tells you about birds and birding.

*A Birdwatcher's Guide to the Eastern United States.* Alice Geffen (Barron's/ paperback). Describes over 700 places to go birding east of the Mississippi River.
*The Habitat Guide to Birding.* Thomas McElroy, Jr. (Knopf). Tells you how to find certain birds according to where they live.
*How to Attract, House and Feed Birds.* Walter Shutz (Collier/ paperback). Gives plans for building bird houses and feeders.
*1001 Questions Answered About Birds.* Allan and Helen Cruickshank. (Dover/ paperback). Full of information and fun.
*Birds in Peril.* John Mackenzie (Houghton Mifflin). A guide to endangered bird species in North America.

# Scorecard

When you have seen and identified a bird, use this scorecard to look up the number of points you have scored.

Before looking up your score, look at the map below, where you will see that North America has been divided into two main regions – Eastern and Western; the Eastern region is the area east of the Rocky Mountains, and the Western region is the remaining area, including the Rocky Mountains. The line running from San Francisco in the West across to Washington D.C. in the East shows the dividing line between North and South, as defined in this book.

There is a separate scorecard for each region, and the birds found in each are arranged in alphabetical order.

A low score means that the bird is common and quite often seen; the highest score is 25, and the higher the score, the rarer the bird. Some birds, like the Crow, are very common throughout North America and therefore have a score of 5 for both regions. Others may be fairly rare in one area and not seen at all in the other (the Orchard Oriole scores 20 in the East but is not found at all in the West).

When you have found your score, you can either ring it in pencil in the book, or you can keep a record of your score in a notebook. Either way you can add up your total score whenever you like.

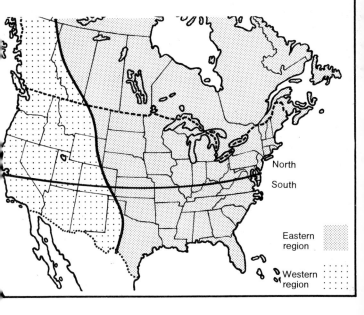

North

South

Eastern region

Western region

# Western Region

| | Score | | Score | | Score |
|---|---|---|---|---|---|
| Auklet, Cassin's | 20 | Dowitcher, Short-billed | 20 | Hawk, Sharp-shinned | 15 |
| Avocet, American | 15 | Duck, Ruddy | 15 | Heron, Black-crowned Night | 15 |
| Blackbird, Red-winged | 5 | Duck, Wood | 20 | Heron, Great Blue | 10 |
| Bluebird, Mountain | 15 | Dunlin | 10 | Heron, Green | 15 |
| Bluebird, Western | 15 | Eagle, Bald | 25 | Hummingbird, Black-chinned | 15 |
| Bobolink | 20 | Egrets, Great and Snowy | 10 | Hummingbird, Rufous | 15 |
| Bobwhite | 10 | Finch, House | 5 | Jaeger, Parasitic | 20 |
| Bufflehead | 15 | Flicker, Common | 10 | Jay, Steller's | 10 |
| Bunting, Lazuli | 15 | Flycatcher, Willow/Alder | 15 | Junco, Dark-eyed | 5 |
| Canvasback | 15 | Gallinule, Common | 15 | Kestrel, American | 10 |
| Cardinal | 15 | Godwit, Marbled | 15 | Killdeer | 10 |
| Catbird, Gray | 10 | Goldfinch, American | 10 | Kingbird, Eastern | 15 |
| Chickadee, Black-capped | 5 | Goose, Canada | 5 | Kingbird, Western | 10 |
| Coot, American | 5 | Goose, Snow/Blue | 15 | Kingfisher, Belted | 10 |
| Cormorant, Double-crested | 5 | Goose, White-fronted | 15 | Kinglet, Golden-crowned | 10 |
| Cowbird, Brown-headed | 10 | Grebe, Pied-billed | 10 | Lark, Horned | 15 |
| Crane, Sandhill | 15 | Grosbeak, Evening | 10 | Loon, Common | 15 |
| Creeper, Brown | 10 | Grouse, Ruffed | 15 | Magpie, Black-billed | 10 |
| Crow, Common | 5 | Grouse, Spruce | 20 | Magpie, Yellow-billed | 15 |
| Cuckoo, Yellow-billed | 15 | Gull, Herring | 5 | Mallard | 5 |
| Dipper | 15 | Gull, Ring-billed | 10 | Martin, Purple | 10 |
| Dove, Mourning | 5 | Hawk, Marsh | 15 | Meadowlark, Eastern | 20 |
| Dove, Rock | 5 | Hawk, Red-tailed | 15 | Meadowlark, Western | 10 |

| | Score | | Score | | Score |
|---|---|---|---|---|---|
| Merganser, Red-breasted | 15 | Robin, American | 5 | Tern, Royal | 20 |
| Mockingbird | 15 | Sanderling | 10 | Thrush, Hermit | 10 |
| Murre, Common | **N**20 **S**25 | Sandpipers, Least and Spotted | 10 | Towhee, Rufous-sided | 10 |
| Murre, Thick-billed | 20 | Sapsucker, Yellow-bellied | 15 | Turnstone, Ruddy | 15 |
| Nighthawk, Common | 15 | Scaup, Lesser | 10 | Veery | 15 |
| Nuthatch, Red-breasted | 15 | Shoveler, Northern | 10 | Vireos, Red-eyed and Solitary | 10 |
| Nuthatch, White-breasted | 10 | Siskin, Pine | 10 | Vulture, Black | 15 |
| Oriole, Northern | 15 | Snipe, Common | 15 | Vulture, Turkey | 10 |
| Osprey | 20 | Sora | 20 | Warbler, Black-and-white | 10 |
| Owl, Great Horned | 20 | Sparrow, Chipping | 10 | Warbler, Wilson's | 10 |
| Owl, Saw-whet | 20 | Sparrow, Fox | 10 | Warbler, Yellow | 10 |
| Owl, Screech | 20 | Sparrow, House | 5 | Warbler, Yellow-rumped | 10 |
| Pelican, Brown | 20 | Sparrow, Song | 10 | Waterthrush, Northern | 10 |
| Phalarope, Northern | 20 | Sparrow, Tree | 10 | Waxwing, Cedar | 15 |
| Pheasant, Ring-necked | 10 | Sparrow, White-crowned | 5 | Whimbrel | 20 |
| Pigeon, Band-tailed | 15 | Sparrow, White-throated | 5 | Whip-poor-will | 15 |
| Pintail | 10 | Starling | 5 | Wigeon, American | 15 |
| Plover, Black-bellied | 15 | Stilt, Black-necked | 10 | Willet | 10 |
| Plover, Semipalmated | 10 | Swallow, Bank | 10 | Woodpecker, Downy | 10 |
| Puffin, Tufted | 20 | Swallows, Barn and Tree | 10 | Woodpecker, Hairy | 5 |
| Quail, California | 10 | Swan, Whistling | 10 | Wren, Bewick's and House | **N**10 **S**20 |
| Rail, Virginia | 20 | Tanager, Western | 15 | Wren, Long-billed Marsh | 15 |
| Raven, Common | 15 | Teal, Blue-winged | 10 | Yellowlegs, Greater | 10 |
| Redstart, American | 10 | Terns, Black and Caspian | 15 | Yellowthroat, Common | 10 |
| Roadrunner | 15 | Tern, Least | 15 | | |

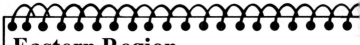

# Eastern Region

| | Score | | Score | | Score |
|---|---|---|---|---|---|
| Blackbird, Red-winged | 5 | Duck, Black | 5 | Grouse. Spruce | 15 |
| Bluebird, Eastern | 15 | Duck, Ruddy | 15 | Gull, Great Black-backed | 10 |
| Bobolink | 15 | Duck, Wood | 15 | Gull, Herring | 5 |
| Bobwhite | 10 | Dunlin | 10 | Gull, Laughing | 10 |
| Brant | 15 | Eagle, Bald | 25 | Gull, Ring-billed | 10 |
| Bufflehead | 15 | Egret, Great | 10 | Hawk, Broad-winged | 15 |
| Bunting, Indigo | 15 | Egret, Snowy | 10 | Hawk, Marsh | 15 |
| Canvasback | 15 | Finch, House | 10 | Hawk, Red-tailed | 15 |
| Cardinal | 5 | Flicker, Common | 10 | Hawk, Sharp-shinned | 15 |
| Catbird, Gray | 10 | Flycatcher, Great Crested | 15 | Heron, Black-crowned Night | 15 |
| Chickadee, Black-capped | 5 | Flycatcher, Willow/Alder | 15 | Heron, Great Blue | 10 |
| Coot, American | 5 | Gallinule, Common | 10 | Heron, Green | 15 |
| Cormorant, Double-crested | 10 | Gannet | 20 | Hummingbird, Ruby-throated | 15 |
| Cowbird, Brown-headed | 10 | Godwit, Marbled | 25 | Ibis, Glossy | 15 |
| Crane, Sandhill | 20 | Goldfinch, American | 10 | Jaeger, Parasitic | 20 |
| Creeper, Brown | 15 | Goose, Canada | 5 | Jay, Blue | 5 |
| Crow, Common | 5 | Goose, Snow/Blue | 15 | Junco, Dark-eyed | 5 |
| Cuckoo, Black-billed | 15 | Goose, White-fronted | 20 | Kestrel, American | 10 |
| Cuckoo, Yellow-billed | 15 | Grackle, Common | 5 | Killdeer | 10 |
| Dickcissel | 15 | Grebe, Pied-billed | 10 | Kingbird, Eastern | 15 |
| Dove, Mourning | 5 | Grosbeak, Evening | 10 | Kingbird, Western | 20 |
| Dove, Rock | 5 | Grosbeak, Rose-breasted | 15 | Kingfisher, Belted | 10 |
| Dowitcher, Short-billed | 15 | Grouse, Ruffed | N15 S25 | Kinglet, Golden-crowned | 10 |

| | Score | | Score | | Score |
|---|---|---|---|---|---|
| Lark, Horned | 15 | Pheasant, Ring-necked | 10 | Sparrow, Song | 10 |
| Loon, Common | 15 | Phoebe, Eastern | 10 | Sparrow, Tree | 10 |
| Magpie, Black-billed | 10 | Pintail | 15 | Sparrow, White-crowned | 10 |
| Mallard | 5 | Plover, Black-bellied | 15 | Sparrow, White-throated | 5 |
| Martin, Purple | 10 | Plover, Semipalmated | 10 | Starling | 5 |
| Meadowlark, Eastern | 10 | Puffin, Common | 25 | Swallow, Bank | 10 |
| Meadowlark, Western | 20 | Rail, Virginia | 20 | Swallow, Barn | 10 |
| Merganser, Red-breasted | 15 | Raven, Common | 20 | Swallow, Tree | 5 |
| Mockingbird | 10 | Razorbill | 20 | Swan, Whistling | N15 S20 |
| Murre, Common | 20 | Redstart, American | 10 | Swift, Chimney | 10 |
| Murre, Thick-billed | 20 | Robin, American | 5 | Tanager, Scarlet | 15 |
| Nighthawk, Common | 15 | Sanderling | 10 | Teal, Blue-winged | 10 |
| Nuthatch, Red-breasted | 15 | Sandpiper, Least | 10 | Tern, Black | 15 |
| Nuthatch, White-breasted | 10 | Sandpiper, Semipalmated | 10 | Tern, Caspian | 15 |
| Oriole, Northern | 15 | Sandpiper, Spotted | 10 | Tern, Common | 10 |
| Oriole, Orchard | 20 | Sapsucker, Yellow-bellied | 15 | Tern, Least | 15 |
| Osprey | 20 | Scaup, Lesser | 10 | Tern, Royal | 15 |
| Owl, Barred | 20 | Shoveler, Northern | 10 | Thrasher, Brown | 10 |
| Owl, Great Horned | 20 | Siskin, Pine | 10 | Thrush, Hermit | 10 |
| Owl, Saw-whet | 20 | Skimmer, Black | 15 | Thrush, Wood | 10 |
| Owl, Screech | 20 | Snipe, Common | 15 | Titmouse, Tufted | 10 |
| Parula, Northern | 15 | Sora | 20 | Towhee, Rufous-sided | 10 |
| Pelican, Brown | 15 | Sparrow, Chipping | 10 | Turkey | N20 S15 |
| Pewee, Eastern Wood | 10 | Sparrow, Fox | 10 | Turnstone, Ruddy | 15 |
| Phalarope, Northern | 20 | Sparrow, House | 5 | Veery | 10 |

| | Score | | Score | | Score |
|---|---|---|---|---|---|
| Vireo, Red-eyed | 10 | | | | |
| Vireo, Solitary | 10 | | | | |
| Vulture, Turkey | 10 | | | | |
| Warbler, Black-and-white | 10 | | | | |
| Warbler, Chestnut-sided | 15 | | | | |
| Warbler, Magnolia | 15 | | | | |
| Warbler, Wilson's | 15 | | | | |
| Warbler, Yellow | 10 | | | | |
| Warbler, Yellow-rumped | 10 | | | | |
| Waterthrush, Northern | 10 | | | | |
| Waxwing, Cedar | 15 | | | | |
| Whimbrel | 20 | | | | |
| Whip-poor-will | 15 | | | | |
| Wigeon, American | 15 | | | | |
| Willet | 10 | | | | |
| Woodcock, American | 15 | | . | | |
| Woodpecker, Downy | 5 | | | | |
| Woodpecker, Hairy | 5 | | | | |
| Woodpecker, Red-bellied | 10 | | | | |
| Wren, Bewick's | 15 | | | | |
| Wren, House | 10 | | | | |
| Wren, Long-billed Marsh | 15 | | | | |
| Yellowlegs, Greater | 10 | | | | |
| Yellowthroat, Common | 10 | | | | |
| | | | | | |

# Glossary

**breeding plumage**-the feathers during the time of mating, nesting and laying eggs.

**camouflage**-when the color of a bird matches its background and makes it difficult to see.

**colony**-group of birds of the same species nesting together.

**conifer (Coniferous)**-trees that bear cones, have needlelike leaves and are usually evergreen. Pines and firs are typical conifers.

**deciduous**-a tree, or any sort of plant, that loses its leaves every year, usually in the fall.

**courtship display**-when a male bird attracts a mate. Some birds show off their plumage; others put on a **display** in the air.

**cover**-places where birds hide, such as thickets, bushes or thick grass.

**habitat**-the particular type of place where a bird lives.

**migration**-the movement of birds from one place to another, usually from their breeding area to one where they spend the winter. A migrating bird is called a migrant, or visitor.

**Molt**-when birds shed their old feathers and grow new ones. All birds do this at least once a year. In ducks, the duller plumage that remains is called **eclipse plumage.**

**Palmated**-refers to a bird's feet, when they are divided like the fingers of a hand.

**Phase**-one of several different plumages that a particular bird has e.g. the Screech Owl.

**Race**-a subspecies; a geographical group of birds that are slightly different from another geographical group within the same species.

**Roost**-to settle in one place for the night. A roost is the name given to a place where birds sleep.

**Species**-a group of birds that all look alike and behave in the same way e.g. Herring Gull is the name of one species.

**Speculum**-a patch of color on a bird's wing, particularly among ducks.

# Index